Gram and the Kids

by Luke Anderson
illustrated by Luanne Marten

Core Decodable 104

I0806541

McGraw Hill Education

Bothell, WA • Chicago, IL • Columbus, OH • New York, NY

MHEonline.com

Send all inquiries to:
McGraw-Hill Education
8787 Orion Place
Columbus, OH 43240-4027

ISBN: 978-0-02-145399-3
MHID: 0-02-145399-3

Printed in the United States of America.

9 10 11 12 KOD 24

Gram stood inside the house. In the yard, the boys made a snow fort. Gram smiled.

The kids would try and retry to make snow walls. But the walls just looked like bumps.

The snow reminded Gram about her dad long ago. He knew how to make a snow fort.

"Pack snow inside a box. The box can make a snow brick." That is what her dad said.

Gram did not like the cold much these days. But she could not stay inside. She wanted to help the boys!

Gram visited the basement to get empty boxes. They had held boots, books, and more stuff. Gram could reuse them.

Gram dressed in a heavy coat, mittens, and hat. "Thin clothes are improper for cold," her dad always said.

The boys were surprised to see Gram. "Let me help you remake that fort," she said.

Could Gram make a fort? That seemed impossible! But Gram grabbed a box and packed snow in it.

Gram used the box to make a snow brick.
Making a fort was not impossible for Gram!

The boys used and reused the boxes to make snow bricks. They stacked bricks on bricks.

Now the boys had a real snow fort! The happy boys each hugged and rehugged Gram.

The boxes were wet now. The boys set them on the porch. Gram would recycle the boxes later.

Later Gram looked out. The boys had printed in the snow "Thanks Gram!" Gram said to herself, "Thanks Dad!"